CAREERS *in Your Community*™

WORKING
as a
AW ENFORCEMENT
OFFICER
in YOUR COMMUNITY

Daniel E. Harmon

New York

Published in 2016 by The Rosen Publishing Group, Inc.
29 East 21st Street, New York, NY 10010

Library of Congress Cataloging-in-Publication Data

Harmon, Daniel E.
Working as a law enforcement officer in your community/Daniel E. Harmon.—First edition.
    pages cm.—(Careers in your community)
Includes bibliographical references and index.
ISBN 978-1-4994-6115-2 (library bound)
1. Police—Juvenile literature. 2. Police—Vocational guidance—Juvenile literature. 3. Law enforcement—Vocational guidance—Juvenile literature. I. Title.
HV7922.H29 2016
363.2023—dc23

                                                    2014047027

Manufactured in the United States of America

Contents

4   *Introduction*

7   **CHAPTER** *One*
Cops on the Beat

19   **CHAPTER** *Two*
Private Eyes

30   **CHAPTER** *Three*
**State Officers Working
Within the Community**

40   **CHAPTER** *Four*
Guarding Prisoners

49   **CHAPTER** *Five*
Securing the Premises

60   **CHAPTER** *Six*
**Community Jobs Related
to Law Enforcement**

68   **Glossary**
69   **For More Information**
73   **For Further Reading**
75   **Bibliography**
78   **Index**

Introduction

A police officer patrolling two blocks away hears the dispatcher's radioed alert, "Bank robbery in progress," and realizes she is the closest responder to the scene. She arrives quickly and positions herself behind cover, intently waiting for the robber to emerge. Her nearest backup is still minutes away.

"Police! Hands in the air!" she shouts, gripping and aiming her semiautomatic weapon in both hands as the ski-masked bandit emerges. He freezes, drops the loot, and surrenders, palms lifted high and opened. With sirens blaring, support units storm onto the scene—finding that she already has the matter well in hand.

"Good work," mutters her captain, impressed.

That kind of scenario happens only on television. But imagine this scene: An elderly man stumbles as he steps into the street at a red traffic light. He tumbles headlong into the lane. As he lies prone—unseen by oncoming drivers—the light turns green. A beat cop who's noticed the accident from a distance rushes to the fallen man's side and shrills an alert to halt traffic.

Community law enforcement officers truly are heroes, but they are rarely the type depicted on television and in film. Still, the heroism they perform regularly is pretty cool.

Most police incidents are nonconfrontational and hardly exciting. The key duties of every officer are to help people and diffuse stressful situations. In times

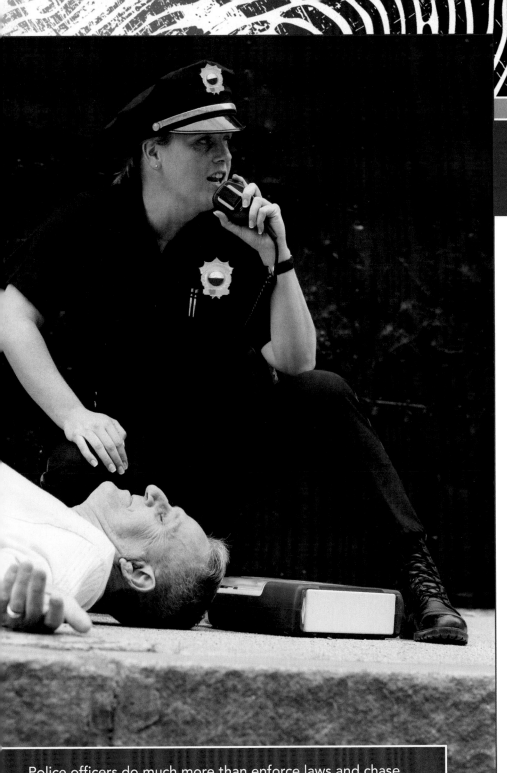

Police officers do much more than enforce laws and chase criminals. They often respond to incidents in which citizens require emergency assistance.

past, police were called peacemakers. Peacekeeping remains their primary purpose.

Law enforcement officers do not work constantly in the line of fire. Days or weeks pass with no violent or threatening incidents in their reports. In some roles, such as village police and industrial security staff, officers rarely if ever fire or even draw their duty weapons.

However, in any law enforcement job, officers must constantly be on alert, prepared for a potentially lethal encounter. Threats usually arise when least expected. A routine traffic stop can become a crisis if a driver has a revoked (or no) license, the vehicle is stolen, or an occupant possesses stolen goods or illegal drugs. A school security officer can never be sure that every student or visitor has no harmful intentions. A wildlife officer checking fishing permits on a lake cannot know what's concealed under a boat seat or inside the tackle box of an unlicensed fisher.

Young career explorers are naturally drawn to the excitement and drama in televised police shows and movies. The greatest reward in law enforcement, though, is community service. A law enforcement career also presents opportunities for professional and personal improvement. Officers stay abreast of advancing technology and hone their computer knowledge. They mature in communication, problem solving, and other skills.

Law enforcement is a challenging career field. In many jobs, dangerous situations arise unpredictably. Shift schedules can be wearisome. Not all citizens appreciate the risks and sacrifices officers make on their behalf. Nevertheless, it is a vocation young people willing to commit to a life of invaluable community service should consider.

CHAPTER One

Cops on the Beat

A woman wakes at 2 AM to the sound of a locked window being forced open. A store window smashing sets off an alarm. Teens on bikes invade a city park, daring one another with reckless tricks in the midst of picnicking families with small children exploring the grounds. An argument between neighbors escalates when each stomps inside for a weapon. Bystanders witness a man dragging a woman from a car and slapping her repeatedly.

Municipal police or county deputies will most likely be the responders to 911 calls about incidents such as these. They are the cops on the beat who protect their communities.

What Police Do

Police are on the front line of protecting life and property. They investigate crimes and apprehend the culprits. Their work is often stressful, dangerous, and physically challenging. Meanwhile, they pro-vide countless deeds of assistance to citizens every

Officers assigned to school patrols get to know students and faculty, establishing a relationship of mutual respect. Students learn that the police are there to protect and help them.

day. They also help educate the public, speaking to groups on safety and drug abuse and instilling an understanding of laws that ensure a better quality of life for everyone.

Police departments strive to work closely with the people of a community. Examples of community services are neighborhood watch programs. Officers meet with small groups and explain how residents can help protect their neighborhoods by looking out for suspicious activities.

Uniformed Officers

Patrolling, uniformed police officers and deputies are responsible for enforcing laws. They look for suspicious activity and apprehend lawbreakers and suspects. In most situations, incidents can be resolved quietly. A simple warning may be appropriate. In other cases, the officer must issue a citation or make an arrest.

In most police cases, violators of minor offenses as well as many major crime suspects surrender willingly. Specially trained teams of law enforcement officers usually apprehend armed and dangerous criminals. However, all police officers are armed and must be prepared to react with force in threatening situations.

Much of an officer's work is preventive: observing the area, identifying potential problems, and taking steps to avert hazards and crises. Police are also trained in first aid. As first responders in many emergency calls, they sometimes save lives.

Officers are assigned to patrol specific areas. They may be dispatched to respond to a call for help—sometimes outside their patrol areas, if other officers are unavailable. In large cities, police often patrol in pairs. In small towns and less populated counties, they usually work alone.

Town and city police are responsible for enforcing all laws, including traffic. County deputies are less engaged in traffic law enforcement. State highway patrol officers, described in a later section, have primary traffic control responsibility outside city limits.

After they gain experience, some officers are trained for special operations. These assignments include canine corps; horseback, bicycle, and

A canine unit inspects a bag that may contain illegal substances. The canine corps is one of several specialty roles in police work.

motorcycle patrols; narcotics units; and SWAT (special weapons and tactics) teams.

When crimes or suspicious activities occur, police obtain warrants to search property or make arrests. They write clear, detailed reports of these actions, which might be questioned in court proceedings later.

Sheriff's deputies serve several special functions in addition to patrolling their counties. They staff county jails and transport prisoners. Some serve as bailiffs, officers assigned to secure a courtroom.

Uniformed police and deputies typically work eight-hour shifts. Newer officers are normally assigned the least popular shifts—nights, weekends, and holidays. Overtime is common.

Detectives

Police detectives, or special agents, investigate crimes or suspected crimes that have occurred. They secure the scenes, carefully collect evidence, inter-view witnesses, and gather facts. They frequently conduct stakeouts, observing the movements of suspects. When they are satisfied that arrests are justified, they obtain the necessary warrants before making arrests or searching a building.

A detective is usually assigned to a small number of cases at a time—sometimes only one. The detective works the case until a suspect is arrested or charges are dropped. In major investigations, two or more detectives might be assigned to the same case.

Detectives are almost always former uniformed officers. Like patrol officers, investigators must handle detailed paperwork. They are often sum-moned to testify at trials.

Law enforcement officers sometimes must serve as counselors. They help people who have been traumatized by violent crimes and accidents.

Dangerous and Sad Work

Police expect that sooner or later, perhaps several times a day, they will need to confront people who are breaking laws. That's what they were hired to do. They are thoroughly trained and prepared for dangerous encounters at any moment.

Occurrences of injury and illness are higher in police work than in most other occupations. Physical injuries may occur during motor vehicle pursuits and altercations with lawbreakers. Sometimes they are exposed to communicable diseases and toxic materials.

Some of their work is heartbreaking. The arrest of a drunk driver may leave a distraught spouse to drive their children home. Bystanders sometimes are caught in a fusillade of bullets from a fleeing criminal. Parents send their children into stores to shoplift. Police at crime scenes must help victims and their families cope with hit-and-runs, drive-by shootings, and other senseless assaults. They may be sent to enforce eviction notices on tenants who no longer can pay their rent because of lost jobs.

Police work is no picnic. But officers find that helping their communities in the ways they do is a highly rewarding form of service.

Personal Traits and Basic Requirements

Police officers working on patrol obviously must be physically fit—strong enough to apprehend offenders. Good stamina and quick reactions are important.

THE ABILITY TO OBSERVE

Sherlock Holmes once explained to his colleague Dr. Watson the reason why Watson was not a good crime solver. "You see," said Holmes, "but you do not observe." As an illustration, he asked the doctor how many steps they mounted to their 221-B Baker Street lodgings each day. Watson could not say. He had seen and walked the stairs more than a thousand times, never observing how many steps there were.

The power of observing details is essential in police work and related jobs. It can alert officers to suspicious individual behavior and odd circumstances in particular locations. It also can be crucial for spotting and avoiding hazards that escape common notice.

Some individuals are inherently observant. Those who aren't might make good law enforcement officers, regardless. A keen sense of observation can be a learned trait. Techniques for sharpening observational skills include the following:

- *Clear your mind of thoughts about what is going on in your life: plans for the weekend, emotional hurt by someone's insult, or daydreams. Learn to focus on the details of your changing surroundings.*

- *Develop your peripheral vision, taking into account what appears in the corner of your eye.*

- *Question why your surroundings are as they are. Why is a window open or a door ajar? Why is a broom propped beside a computer workstation? Why is a car parked on the street in front of a home when there's plenty of space in the driveway?*

- *Apply all your senses: vision, hearing, smell, and touch.*

They need good judgment and the ability to reach decisions and resolve problems quickly. Keen perception is needed to understand why individuals take certain actions and to foresee how they might respond in tense situations.

Police are perceived as community leaders. As such, they must take care to protect their image. They must be excellent communicators, whether they are interacting with the public or writing clear reports. Patience, calmness, and empathy are vital characteristics. While they must always be firm in upholding the law, they must also try to understand different people's perspectives and attempt to diffuse potentially troublesome situations.

Most departments require officers to be at least twenty-one years old. They must be U.S. citizens,

Walkie-talkies are still used by patrol officers, but they are considered old school. Today's police also use state-of-the-art technology to make their work more effective and efficient.

have driver's licenses, and be able to pass physical examinations, including drug tests, as well as written assessments.

Education and Training

Some police officers have high school diplomas. Others have associate's degrees. Some have bachelor's, master's, and even doctoral degrees. Degree fields range from criminal justice and law enforcement to psychology or statistics.

New hires must graduate from a law enforcement training academy, then receive on-the-job training. Large departments run their own academies, but most community officers attend their state's police academy. Training may take three months or longer. Classroom instruction covers state and local laws as well as constitutional law. Classes also teach ethics and civil rights.

Outside the classroom, recruits are taught to perform different types of patrols and to direct traffic. They are instructed in self-defense and emergency response. They are trained to use firearms, Tasers, batons, sprays, handcuffs, and other equipment vital for arrests and defense. Recruits learn to use radios, digital cameras and video cameras, dedicated mobile phones, and laptop computers, as well as radar and other detection equipment. Police work in the digital age requires technological skills, including a solid knowledge of online information gathering and communications. Officers use crime mapping and database collections such as the Integrated Automated Fingerprint Identification System maintained by the Federal Bureau of Investigation.

A stint in the military after high school is a smart first step toward an ultimate career in law enforcement. Some military police officers go into police work after their discharge from active duty.

High school students interested in law enforcement careers should take as many classes as they can that might be useful on the job. Helpful subjects include computers, surveillance equipment, and foreign languages.

Career Prospects

By 2022, the U.S. Bureau of Labor Statistics projects that the number of police and detective jobs will increase by about 5 percent from 2012. This is slower than the average growth rate for all occupations. The reason is that although the need for public safety will continue, most state and local government budgets are tightly constrained.

Prospects for entering the police workforce are enhanced for applicants who have served in the military and/or speak a second language. In typical departments, new officers work through an initial (paid) probationary period of at least ninety days. This period of evaluation enables supervisors to rate their skills, competence, and fitness for the job. It also gives new officers time to learn the job thoroughly. Afterward, they enter regular service. They gradually qualify for promotion to corporal, sergeant, lieutenant, and captain.

Experienced officers may qualify for promotion to detective or for special assignments. Advancement opportunities are greatest for officers with bachelor's degrees, investigative experience, and advanced training.

On average, police pay is somewhat higher than for most jobs. Salaries generally are highest for criminal investigators and detectives. Police officers in most organizations receive excellent job benefits and early retirement options.

CHAPTER *Two*

Private Eyes

Friday night is time for weekend unwinding, especially among students. But in one college town, a woman and man entering a pub several blocks off campus don't appear to be in a party mood. The woman is middle aged, conservatively dressed, her brown hair streaked with gray. Her powerfully built, casually clad companion is perhaps a decade younger. They separate and begin circulating through the throng of young people seated at tables and crowded along the bar.

"Have you seen her?" they ask, showing photographs of a pretty, smiling young woman.

The young woman in the pictures is the older woman's daughter; she has been missing for three months. She was last seen standing on the sidewalk outside a bar nearby. The man is a private detective hired by the family to help solve the mystery of her disappearance. Police investigators have done all they can. They continue to follow up on the dwindling number of tips they receive concerning the student's fate. But they don't have time to do what the parents and the detective are doing: canvass the entertainment district night after night, hoping someone has information.

This private investigator (PI, or "private eye") does not earn a lavish income. When he divides his fee by the number of hours he devotes on behalf of clients, he sometimes hardly makes minimum wage. "I eat a lot of ramen noodles," he confides with a chuckle.

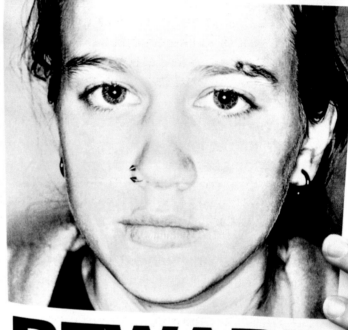

Private investigators are sometimes hired by families to locate missing relatives after the police have exhausted all leads in the case.

He's in it for reasons other than wealth. He's dedicated to helping clients obtain justice when the police, with limited personnel and time, reach dead ends. Missing person cases are his specialty.

He has been rewarded with success in the past. But this investigation—one of thousands of cases of missing persons that have sinister indications—does not have a happy ending. Years go by, and the young woman is not found.

Such is the career of a private investigator. Much of the PI's work is like official detective work. But for the most part, private detectives delve into aspects of law enforcement and legal matters that government detectives don't.

Much Work, Little Glamour

A career as a private law enforcement professional might seem more appealing than that of an officer employed by a local police force. It's true that private eyes are free to set their own hours and fees and accept only those cases that interest them. Instead of patrolling the same daily beat and following routines, they can work on a variety of cases.

But most private investigative work is far from glamorous. Private investigators are called on to perform types of investigations that the regular police do not handle. They are not actually involved in law enforcement—although their work often results in capturing or exposing criminals and solving crimes. They do not make arrests other than a citizen's arrest, which anyone can perform. Generally, their job is to investigate and furnish their clients with information.

Stakeouts are common duties of private eyes. They stealthily observe suspects and locations from a distance, perhaps for hours or even days on end.

PIs are often hired to find evidence for individuals who suspect a spouse is committing adultery. Separated or divorced parents engage them to look into possible child custody violations. Parents pay them to find runaway children. Insurance companies hire them to observe policyholders who might be faking injury claims. Employers need them to observe the behavior of employees who may be stealing or dealing drugs on the job.

To investigate those kinds of matters, PIs find themselves on stakeouts at all hours. On many of these long, dreary vigils, they discover nothing. The work can be quite boring for days at a time.

PIs frequently work evenings and weekends, contacting and interviewing people away from the workplace. They may have to work outdoors in inclement weather. Other work is done in offices, conducting computer research and telephone interviews.

Private detectives often work with clients in very stressful circumstances. For the most part, the work is not especially dangerous and does not require them to be armed. PIs who are hired as bodyguards, however, typically are armed and are prepared for physical confrontations.

Sleuthing with Limited Authority

Private investigators are hired by individuals or companies to collect and preserve evidence that the client could use in a court proceeding. Like police detectives, they interview people who may have relevant information and pore through related records. They conduct surveillance. In certain situations, detectives go undercover—a potentially dangerous quest. If the evidence they obtain is presented in court, they may be called to testify.

A private agent secretly photographs a target. Images and videos of suspects' activities may be presented as evidence at trial.

To obtain evidence, they use a variety of tools, many of which are computers and digital devices. Technology allows them to find phone numbers, addresses, and other facts quickly.

WANT TO BE A PI? FORGET THE ACTION FICTION

Young people for generations have been fascinated by the adventures of fictitious private detectives. Some of the most famous are teenage sleuths: the Hardy Boys and Nancy Drew.

Classic adult mystery stories are still popular. They include Sherlock Holmes (created by Arthur Conan Doyle), Hercule Poirot and Miss Marple (Agatha Christie), Father Brown (G. K. Chesterton), Uncle Abner (Melville Davisson Post), Lady Molly of Scotland Yard (the Baroness Orczy), and the Thinking Machine (Jacques Futrelle). Readers are amazed by each detective's cleverness in spotting obscure clues. Most of the cases are sensational—poisonings, million-dollar jewel heists, espionage, or international smuggling rings.

One thing scarcely mentioned in the stories and novels is the drudgery of detective work: sifting through records, interviewing dozens of people (most of whom have no helpful information), and struggling to stay awake night after night on fruitless stakeouts.

To get an idea of the kinds of assignments detectives actually take on, visit the websites of PI firms. Examine the services they offer to help decide whether the work is what you have in mind.

Despite any dangers they might encounter, such as during confrontations, they operate with no official police power. In the eyes of the law, they are private citizens, nothing more. But they must have a solid understanding of federal, state, and local laws. If they fail to comply with any laws, the evidence they obtain may be useless in court.

Personal Traits of a Good PI

Like government detectives, private eyes require a special combination of personal qualities. The main characteristics are as follows:

- **Inquisitiveness:** *Detectives ask questions and are determined to learn the truth.*

- **Communication skills:** *Contacting and interviewing clients, witnesses, and other information sources is a large part of the job.*

- **Resourcefulness:** *Investigators often begin with scant leads. They must be able to develop and expand them. They look for the most effective avenues for discovering information about persons of interest.*

- **Decision-making skills:** *Investigators must often make quick decisions.*

- **Patience:** *Many investigations are conducted over a long period of time, with little progress from day to day. Veteran PIs know that for all their efforts, some cases will never be resolved satisfactorily.*

Training and Experience

Age is not a major factor in determining a person's qualifications for work as a private investigator. In many states, you theoretically can be a PI as young as eighteen—but only with extensive experience and training, which few eighteen-year-olds have had time to acquire. Most private investigators are former police officers with years of experience.

In California, for example, eighteen is the minimum age for obtaining a license as a private investigator. But in addition, the state's Bureau of Security and Investigative Services stipulates on its online FAQ page that an applicant needs "three years of compensated experience totaling not less than 6,000 hours in investigative work, while employed by law enforcement agencies, collection agencies, insurance agencies, banks, courts, and other private investigation agencies, etc."

There is an exception to the requirement: "A college degree in criminal law, criminal justice, or police science can be substituted for part of the experience." But forget being a Hardy Boy or Nancy Drew. You'll be in your twenties before you can hand out your card as a qualified private eye.

Private investigators are licensed by state law enforcement agencies. A few are comparatively new to law enforcement, but most have years of experience. Law enforcement experience is more important in job hunting than an advanced education, although a two- or four-year degree in criminal justice or police science is required for some agency positions. Some corporate investigators have studied finance, accounting, business, and/or management. Those who investigate cybercrimes need computer training. Continuing

Nancy Drew has long been a popular teenage sleuth of fiction. There are no Nancy Drews in real life—but students can begin preparing for a law enforcement career.

education—learning new computer skills as technology advances—is important for them.

Most investigative and other skills are learned on the job. Naturally, advancement opportunities improve with experience.

A private investigation license is required in most states. An additional license may be required for bodyguard service. Investigators who carry handguns must take firearms training and obtain state permits.

Certification is not required by PIs, but it can be useful for job searching and career advancement. ASIS International and the National Association of Legal Investigators offer certification programs.

Career Prospects

Most private investigators earn at or a little above the average income for all occupations. Most of

WHAT PRIVATE INVESTIGATORS CAN AND CANNOT DO

Private investigators do not have the same legal authority as their counterparts with an official police force. The California Bureau of Security and Investigative Services outlines the essential cans and can'ts at its website's FAQ page. Besides generally investigating matters for private clients, here are examples of things a PI in California can do:

- *Carry a weapon on duty if he or she has state-approved permits for exposed and concealed firearms.* Active-duty peace officers and retired peace officers who have permits can also carry weapons on duty as private investigators.

- *Serve as a bodyguard.* This can only be done, though, in connection with a case to which the PI previously was assigned.

Among things a PI license in California does not authorize are these:

- *Claiming to be an "official" police representative.*

- *Entering a property without the owner's consent.*

- *Wearing a badge. A badge may mislead the public to believe the investigator is an official peace officer or other government official.*

The California bureau makes it clear that a PI "has no law enforcement authority even if he/she has been hired by law enforcement to perform an investigation. A Private Investigator is an ordinary citizen and can only make citizen's arrests."

the best-paying jobs are related to the finance and insurance industries.

Job growth in this field is expected to be about 11 percent between now and 2022. This is approximately the average for all job fields and is slightly higher than the rate for government police. Stimulating growth are increased concerns for securing physical property and, especially, confidential information. Many private agencies now specialize in probing cybercrimes.

Most entry-level jobs are with private detective agencies. Competition for advanced positions is stiff since many applicants are experienced law enforcement and military veterans.

State Officers Working Within the Community

Most community law enforcement officers work for town, city, or county agencies. Some, though, work for state government organizations. They safeguard the health and welfare of different locales in special ways.

The two most common types of community law enforcement officers performing special duties are wildlife and highway patrol professionals. They are community law enforcement officers in the sense that although they are employed by larger (usually state) agencies, they are assigned to work within communities. They typically live in the communities in which they work.

Patrolling the Highways

Highway patrol officers, or state troopers, are responsible for enforcing traffic laws. They patrol state highways and roads along with interstate routes. However, they are trained as police officers, have the same authority, and perform some of the same duties. Troopers may be assigned to assist other police

State troopers are primarily responsible for enforcing traffic laws and promoting highway safety. They are assigned to specific counties but are often dispatched to distant parts of the state.

agencies in different parts of the state. They often respond to dispatcher calls in rural areas.

Like police and deputies, highway patrol officers issue citations, make arrests, and write reports that may be needed in court. Their work is especially dangerous because it involves apprehending speeding motorists and drunk and reckless drivers. Any traffic stop at a roadside poses safety risks. High-speed pursuits of violators who try to get away often end in collisions.

A routine task of traffic police is setting up radar checks to deter speeding. Officers running speed checks often work in pairs or teams.

State and national park rangers protect designated natural and historic properties. Besides enforcing laws and park policies, they provide educational programs and tours.

In the near future, troopers will probably be using more than speed detection technology to make the roads safer. Electronics engineers have developed a radar-like device that can detect texting while driving. The texting gun can distinguish texting signals from other electronic signals. At this writing, it is still in the trial stage. If it proves effective, future technology may become even more diverse—sensing, for example, unbuckled seatbelts.

Besides enforcing laws, highway patrol officers spend much of their time helping motorists. They assist travelers stranded at roadsides and usually are the first responders at accident scenes. Officers investigate and report apparent accident causes.

The necessary skills of state troopers are basically the same as those of other types of law enforcers. Keen perception of detail is particularly important. Highway patrol officers must be able to identify vehicle makes, models, and approximate ages. Excellent vision is a must for reading license tags at a distance. They have to be able to judge the approximate speed of oncoming vehicles.

Policing the Great Outdoors

Fish and game wardens are sometimes referred to as wildlife officers, wildlife conservation officers, or natural resource officers. Their main task is to enforce boating, fishing, and hunting laws. They police the waters and woods of their assigned communities. Officers patrol in different types of vehicles. Some patrol on foot or horseback. In coastal states, some officers police the waters offshore.

SPECIAL TRAINING FOR SPECIAL ROLES

Most wildlife officers receive specialized training in addition to the standard criminal justice training provided by state police academies. In South Carolina, for instance, new city police, county deputies, state troopers, and wildlife officers take the same basic twelve-week program. It includes instruction in criminal law, patrol car driving, firearms instruction, and much more. Afterward, wildlife officers and state troopers have more training in store.

Wildlife officers undergo another eight weeks of training specific to their job. It includes three weeks of boating instruction as well as guidance in wildlife laws, identification, search-and-rescue operations, and man tracking.

An interesting category of training deals

ildlife officers enforce fish and game ws. They are also called in to resolve oblems between humans and wild imals, which may require capturing and ocating dangerous species.

with nuisance wildlife. Trainees have to learn, for example, how to subdue alligators. "In some parts of the state where alligators are prevalent," explains officer Brian Welch, "we are the ones they call when an alligator becomes a nuisance. We have to know how to catch and relocate the animals. Every officer has to subdue an alligator during training." Wildlife officers are also the professionals typically called to resolve reports of suspected rabid animals.

An applicant for his or her state's Department of Natural Resources needs a four-year degree or a two-year degree augmented by three years of related experience. The degree field can be varied, although criminal justice or wildlife-related studies are most common. Welch obtained a bachelor's degree in environmental and natural resources with a minor in biological sciences.

"The process to get hired is lengthy," he says. "It involves an initial interview, physical fitness exams, swimming and written tests, additional interviews, and background interviews."

A common activity is checking fishing and hunting licenses and issuing citations for violations. But wildlife officers do much more. They can arrest sportsmen for boating while under the influence of alcohol or drugs. They investigate landowners' complaints. They frequently encounter serious offenses such as night hunting or hunting out of season. Violators often flee and, on occasion, violently resist arrest.

Officers lead or join in search-and-rescue operations. They are invited to schools and community meetings to educate students and the general public about outdoor laws and safety. In some states, wildlife officers conduct hunter education programs and manage firing ranges. They collect ecological data about the conditions of various wildlife species.

Brian Welch, a Department of Natural Resources officer in South Carolina, points out that the job is never the same from day to day. "Throughout the year, the job changes with the seasons. In the springtime, people are out getting their boats ready, turkey hunting, and beginning to fish. In the summer, increased recreational boating takes over and you have a lot of responsibilities on the lakes. During the fall and winter, an officer's duties change to focus on the majority of the hunting seasons, including dove, ducks, deer, and bear."

Welch observes that training never ends. "We have multiple training periods throughout the year to qualify to use vehicles and firearms. You also become qualified in alcohol and drug detection and receive training on this yearly."

Officers serve as the primary agents for enforcing boating laws. They are also in the front lines of homeland security. "We have the equipment and knowledge to patrol nuclear facilities and shipments and ports."

In Welch's state, wildlife officers have statewide jurisdiction but are assigned to work in a particular county. They enforce federal as well as state wildlife laws, and they are authorized to enforce any state criminal law. They occasionally arrest traffic violators.

The fact that they work alone, in remote areas, makes their work "very different from [that of] a regular police officer," Welch points out. "Our backup is usually far away and everyone we encounter is almost always armed with a gun or knife. It can be dangerous work.

"It is very common to be doing a routine check on hunters or fishers and find them in possession of drugs, have a warrant out for their arrest, or find out they are not actually hunting or fishing but trespassing to steal scrap metal or commit burglary. Many times I have stopped to check on a person or truck that I thought was engaged in hunting, and it turned into a burglary, sale of narcotics, stolen vehicle, or domestic violence situation. As state officers, we have to be prepared to deal with these situations accordingly."

Welch enthuses that the job—for all its isolation, stress, and danger—is highly rewarding. "I would encourage any teenager who has an interest in the outdoors, the community, and law enforcement to look into this career. I can think of no better office than the areas we get to see daily. Nor can I think of any job where you might teach a young child about boating safety or give a career day presentation at a high school in the morning, check people hunting or fishing in the afternoon and evening, and then receive a call at midnight about a stranded boater or person lost in the woods who is possibly injured."

Career Preparation and Job Prospects

Personal traits, educational requirements, and preliminary training are basically the same for state law enforcement officers as for county sheriff's deputies and municipal police. They receive additional instruction in the aspects of law enforcement that pertain specifically to their jobs. In some states, associate's or bachelor's degrees are required for state trooper and wildlife officer candidates.

Jobs as park rangers appeal especially to people who love the outdoors. They are dedicated to protecting the surroundings they enjoy.

While in high school, students who are interested in wildlife careers—whether in law enforcement, conservation, or scientific studies—can begin focused preparation. They should apply themselves especially in biology and chemistry classes. If available, elective Earth science courses, clubs, or projects will provide additional groundwork for a career.

Wildlife officers earn approximately as much as community police officers and deputies. Highway patrol officers in some states are paid more. The growth rate for trooper positions is expected to be about the same as that for police; the rate for wildlife officer jobs may be slower.

Seasoned highway patrol officers are promoted through the ranks. Typically, they begin as troopers and advance to corporal, sergeant, lieutenant, captain, major, lieutenant colonel, and colonel.

Guarding Prisoners

Correctional officers enforce rules and prevent problems among inmates at city and county jails and detention centers as well as at state and federal prisons. They monitor inmate activities inside the facilities and guard the perimeters against escapes. In addition, they perform routine duties such as inspecting the buildings and screening authorized individuals who enter and exit.

Most community jobs in corrections are at municipal jails or larger county detention centers. Those facilities are designed to house prisoners who have been sentenced to relatively short terms of incarceration (typically ninety days or fewer). Convicted criminals sentenced to longer terms are sent to prison. Prison facilities are located in communities throughout each state. Correctional officer jobs are available to trained professionals who live in those communities.

State correctional institutions are designed to house different categories of inmates. Inmates who are considered to pose little threat to prison staff and to society are placed in minimum-security facilities.

Trained officers maintain order and safety inside jails and prisons of different security levels. Interestingly, most guards who work inside a prison are unarmed.

They have few restraints inside the prison, which is enclosed by basic (but adequate) fencing. At many minimum-security prisons, certain inmates earn the freedom to work under supervision in regular jobs throughout the community.

Medium-security prisons house inmates serving longer terms. Some but not all prisoners are considered dangerous. These facilities guard individuals who have committed violent crimes as well as long-term inmates found guilty of lesser offenses. Violent inmates are housed apart from the others.

Maximum-security institutions contain prisoners who are considered very dangerous to society. Inmates are confined in individual cells. The facilities are surrounded by layered fencing of different types including razor wire.

Prisoners are often transferred to different facilities. Some inmates who face life sentences may begin their sentences in heavily guarded prisons but eventually be transferred to less restricted locations if they exhibit good behavior. Meanwhile, a prisoner in a minimum-security institution may be moved into more closely guarded confinement if he or she commits a crime while incarcerated. Prisoners may also be transferred because of housing limitations.

Guard Duty

A prison dormitory in a low-security institution may house a hundred or more inmates. The typical routine of a night guard begins by observing them during dinner and afterward, signaling "lights out" (turning off the TV and lights in common areas) at the scheduled time, and maintaining surveillance over the dormitory all night.

UNARMED GUARDS

Action films make it seem like all prison guards are heavily armed. In the movies, guards often tote military-grade automatic rifles, sidearms, and assorted lethal and nonlethal weapons. In reality, guards do not carry firearms inside the grounds, where they come into direct contact with prisoners. In the event of a riot or uprising, armed guards could be overwhelmed and their weapons confiscated by inmates.

For the most part, armed guards survey the grounds from observation towers and patrol the perimeter. They are trained in the use of various weapons, including shotguns and rifles. When violence erupts inside the prison, specially trained forces are called in to respond.

Guards wake the inmates in the morning and send them to breakfast. Shortly afterward, the day shift arrives to relieve the night officers.

Regular duties include inspecting inmates and their living quarters. Guards look and feel under the sink and around the toilet and bed. They search for any item that does not belong there and report their findings. Guards examine doors and window bars for evidence of tampering. They inspect incoming mail and screen visitors.

Throughout the day, correctional officers enforce prison rules. Prisoners are restricted from certain areas or are allowed to enter them only at certain

A prison warden *(left)* confers with a correctional officer. Wardens earn the respect of both staff and inmates by taking a personal interest in daily routines.

times. They must not abuse privileges they are given, such as television and music. Guards supervise their activities and must know where each inmate is at all times. They break up arguments and assaults among prisoners.

When inmates break the rules, guards impose a progressive series of sanctions. Sanctions usually involve a temporary loss of privileges.

NOTES FROM A PRISON GUARD

Michael Waid already had experience as a security officer in the retail and industrial sectors when he joined the force at a medium-security prison in South Carolina. He was also a National Guard veteran who served a tour of duty as a military police officer in Afghanistan.

In addition to his years of experience, he underwent a month of full-time training for the state correctional officer job. It encompassed all the skills a guard might need, from restraint procedures to firearms operation to life-saving techniques.

Next he began on-the-job orientation by shadowing a veteran officer to give him a feel for the job. He was then assigned for two months to monitor and patrol the "easy dorms," where nonviolent inmates rarely caused disturbances. Later, he was assigned to guard areas where more aggressive inmates were housed. During his three years at the facility, the most violent incident was a prolonged fight among inmates in the exercise yard. Guards brought it under control with pepper spray.

Waid observes that guards are thoroughly trained before they're assigned to any post. They are never placed in situations in which they don't know what to do when an incident occurs.

His daily contact with prisoners posed no serious dangers. "But you have to be assertive. You have to be a stickler for the rules. They'll push the rules because they have nothing else to do."

Waid considers corrections "a good career to get into. As long as there's a government, there will be prisons."

In some facilities, prisoners must be secured with handcuffs and leg irons for transportation to a courthouse or other outside destination. Some prisoners are restrained inside when being taken to meet visitors.

Correctional officers also assist inmates. They facilitate counseling, educational sessions, and work assignments.

For the most part, work conditions are comfortable. Some officers, however, work outside in all seasons or in areas of the prison that are not temperature controlled. Some facilities are overcrowded, poorly ventilated, and very noisy. Officers may have to stand or sit for long periods. They generally work in eight-hour shifts, but twelve-hour rotations may be scheduled. Prisons are staffed twenty-four hours a day, seven days a week, even on holidays. The turnover rate among correctional officers is fairly high because of the hours and job-related stress.

Correctional officers have a high rate of injury and illness. They may be injured in physical confrontations with prisoners. Contagious diseases spread easily in crowded institutions, such as prisons.

Personal Traits

Correctional officers need good communication and interpersonal skills and the ability to defuse troublesome situations before they get out of control. They must have good judgment for quickly assessing a problem and deciding on a course of action. Officers need to be resourceful, finding the best way to resolve a developing situation. They need self-discipline to remain calm and control their emotions in the face of hostility.

Correctional officers may provide counseling to inmates. They resolve problems among prisoners and diffuse potentially dangerous situations before they escalate into crises.

Officers must be physically fit. They may be required to subdue resisting or violent prisoners.

Education and Training

A high school diploma or GED (general equivalency degree) is enough for most correctional facility jobs. Applicants must be at least age eighteen (twenty-one for some jobs), must be U.S. citizens or permanent residents, and must not be convicted felons.

Training takes place at state-run academies. Recruits learn the regulations and operational policies of the institution. They are trained in taking custody of inmates, handling security, and self-defense. Most guards are unarmed, but they may be trained in fire-arms use at the academy.

After completing the academy program, new guards receive on-the-job training at the facility where they will work. This period lasts from several weeks to several months.

Career Prospects

Sadly, there will always be a need for correctional facilities and officers to run them. Federal, state, or county governments run most prisons and jails. A recent trend in the correctional industry has been that governments contract with private companies to operate prisons. Thus, jobs are available with both government agencies and security companies. However, the overall job growth rate is expected to be just 5 percent by 2022, slower than the average growth rate for all jobs.

Promotion within the prison system could lead to a position as correctional sergeant, overseeing the guard staff. Beyond that, experienced officers can rise to become supervisors and administrators. The highest position at a prison is that of warden.

On average, correctional officers earn consid-erably less than police officers and detectives. The highest salaries are for administrators and officers with long experience.

CHAPTER Five

Securing the Premises

While correctional officers keep close watch on people, security officers primarily guard property. Security officers work in different communities at factories, wholesale distribution centers, banks, office buildings, shopping malls, and hotels. They also secure airports, hospitals, schools, and other public institutions.

Some security personnel monitor buildings and grounds from control rooms, observing scenes recorded by video cameras. They direct ground officers to areas of suspicious activity.

Security personnel watch for theft—by employees as well as customers and visitors. They protect against other illegal activities ranging from vandalism to terrorism. In this way, they help make their communities safer places to live.

Wide-Ranging Roles

A job in security is an excellent starting point for a young person interested in law enforcement. It is not a high-paying vocation, and few make it a lifelong career. But for teenagers and young adults exploring the job market—including recent high school graduates and college students—it is a fairly easy field to enter. It provides preliminary insights into the work of professionals dedicated to protecting life and property. And it is an impressive credential for pursuing other areas of law enforcement.

Commercial and Business Security Officers

These officers watch financial, retail, wholesale, industrial, and private office locations. They note and report unusual activity. When serious incidents occur, they rarely attempt to make arrests. Usually, they notify the police or other emergency responders (ambulance and fire services).

At some locations, security personnel are hired to control the coming and going of visitors and employees. They check photo IDs, monitor people passing through electronic screening stations, and search through handbags that do not pass through the screens. If the screening gate sets off an alarm, the

Officers at airport terminals and other screening stations inspect baggage. They wear gloves mainly as sanitary precautions, protecting them from harmful germs that may be present.

person passing through is subjected to a more sensitive scan with an electronic wand.

Some officers observe activities on surveillance cameras. Officers also patrol facilities, observing doors, restrooms, and other checkpoints for possible security breaches. They radio information of suspicious findings to control centers. Written reports are required for certain incidents.

Security Personnel at Public Sites

Officers at universities, schools, and office complexes look for suspicious activities and circumstances inside and out. In large libraries, museums, and galleries, they keep an eye on patrons and check through briefcases and bags of people departing the building. At concerts and sporting events, officers supervise seating and direct parking and traffic. As at business and industrial locations, they check the credentials of people entering restricted areas.

Many security officers at schools and public events are law enforcement professionals. Uniformed police or deputies in some communities are on special assignment guarding schools. Off duty, many police officers moonlight working security at ball games, concerts, festivals, and fairs.

Store Detectives

Large retail stores hire loss prevention agents, commonly known as store detectives. Their essential duty is to prevent shoplifting. They also watch for theft by store employees.

Store detectives in large department stores work from camera rooms, monitoring floor activities revealed by surveillance cameras. They pay particular attention to customers who appear less concerned with examining products than they are with their surroundings—peering into areas of the ceiling to locate cameras or turning away when sales staff approach. Agents also patrol the store interior and parking lot on foot. They try to recover pilfered merchandise or prevent shoplifters from leaving the premises until police arrive. (Agents may be limited in their powers of arrest and detention.)

To prevent employee theft, agents check register transactions. They look for a pattern of markdowns, a sign that an employee may be giving unauthorized discounts to friends or relatives.

Working for Security Agencies

Typically, security personnel do not work directly for the businesses and community institutions they guard. Most businesses, industries, and organizations contract with a security agency to provide services and staff. Security officers are hired by the agency. They may be assigned to work at one location for an extended period, or they may be assigned to different locations in the area.

At local institutions that are affiliated with state governments, job applications are often processed through the state employment office. State or local police provide security at many government facilities. At others, it is handled by a security agency under contract with the government. Universities and colleges with resident student housing typically have their own campus security forces.

Dramatic Encounters, Dull Routines

Most security officers are unarmed. Even armed guards assigned to banks and other prime target locations rarely use their weapons. They are stationed at such sites essentially as deterrents and observers. They summon police when crimes occur or serious threats arise.

"Security is mainly a physical presence," explains Michael Waid, who has worked as both a security officer and prison guard. "If anything happens, you call the people who need to know—your supervisor or the employer."

Report writing is a wearisome but necessary part of security work. Officers make notes of the routine tasks they perform and unusual findings.

For making arrests, security officers in most states have only the universal authority of citizen's arrest. In some states, security personnel are tested and licensed by a state law enforcement agency. They have the same arrest power as a deputy (though only at the locations where they are assigned).

Like regular police, security personnel must make regular reports. It's a task many officers disdain, but it is vital. Officers write incident reports and make patrol notes that may be useful in investigations.

NEVER OFF DUTY

A common syndrome among security officers is that they find themselves "always on." The essence of what they are trained to do while on duty is to observe the people and circumstances around them. When they go off duty, it isn't a simple matter to drop their vigilance and totally relax.

Veteran security personnel confide that when they go out to dinner or attend social events with spouses, dates, or groups of friends, their companions complain that they seem disconnected. They very well may be a bit out of touch. They instinctively observe the behavior of others in the room.

This isn't a bad trait to have. Self-improvement and motivational consultants point out that sharpening powers of observation is a worthwhile exercise for anyone. Jobs in security and other community law enforcement roles are excellent for honing those skills.

Officers are encouraged to become acquainted with the people who are around them regularly. Besides other officers they work with, this includes managers and employees of the client company. Officers learn to recognize outside contractors, snack room vendors, delivery personnel, law enforcement officers who patrol the area, and others who frequently enter and exit the property. They pay extra attention to newcomers, even if the strangers carry credentials.

"It's a stable job," Waid says. "It's easy to get into if you have a good background. And it's really good to have on your résumé, even if you do that for only a year or so.

Law enforcement and security officers get to know the people with whom they come in regular contact. Here, an officer at a school chats with students.

"It can be tedious and repetitive. The hours can be long. You might sit a lot, and then you patrol. It is a fairly easy job, but you have to be professional."

Important Personal Qualities and Skills

Security officers are constantly on alert and have to pay close attention to detail. They must be able to make quick decisions, including arresting a suspect. A firm but calm demeanor is needed when encountering individuals who may be violating laws or employer policies. Officers must communicate clearly with both suspected

Security and police work sometimes requires officers to be outside in harsh and dangerous weather conditions. Physical fitness and stamina are important qualities.

violators and law enforcement personnel who are called to the scene. They must work well with teams and be able to function confidently when patrolling alone.

Physically, stamina is an underlying requirement. Security officers spend a lot of time on their feet, standing at guard posts or walking on patrol for hours at a time. They sometimes work outside in inclement weather or inside buildings without temperature controls. They must have good vision (it may be corrected vision) and be able to understand voice transmissions on static-plagued radios and amid background noise.

Technological skills are essential for many security positions. Officers engaged in electronic surveillance must know how to operate the equipment and evaluate results. Officers on patrol use electronic devices to test checkpoints and make reports.

A criminal background check and drug testing are required. Credit checks are usually required for loss prevention agents.

Education and Training

Applicants for most security jobs must be at least eighteen years old and have a driver's license. A high school diploma or GED (general equivalency degree) suffices for most jobs. Some security agencies require or prefer secondary education in criminal justice or police science. Most top-level security supervisors have a two- or four-year degree plus several years of experience. Many security personnel are military veterans.

Training varies greatly. Typically, security companies provide initial orientation. Classroom sessions may last one or two days. They explain job duties, basic criminal and civil law, safety and emergency procedures, dealing with suspected violators, job regulations and ethics, powers of search and arrest, patrol and screening functions, and report writing. This stage of training usually includes testing for registration with the state's law enforcement bureau.

Recruits then begin learning their specific duties on the job. On-the-job training may take two days or longer. Large national and international security companies maintain training schools for employees who will be serving in advanced security positions.

Career Prospects

The outlook for job openings in the security field is bright. Demand for security services is growing steadily. At the same time, turnover is fairly high. Because of the generally low pay (some entry-level jobs pay only minimum wage), many people take jobs in security only until they find more lucrative work.

Career security professionals in higher-paying, supervisory jobs typically have years of experience. Many of them are former law enforcement officers. Those who have postsecondary education and qualify as armed guards have the best opportunities for advancement.

Community Jobs Related
to Law Enforcement

Numerous jobs are linked to law enforcement and criminal justice. Some are part of separate but parallel career areas. Others represent unique categories of law enforcement. The jobs are wide ranging. Some require degrees in criminal justice, psychology, social work, or specialized programs. Others require only a GED.

Probation Officers

Probation officers are also known as community supervision officers. They oversee the activities of criminal offenders who have been sentenced to terms of probation rather than prison sentences. Their job is to see that each offender is rehabilitated and poses no threat to the community. They meet regularly with each person and with the individual's family and write progress reports. They sometimes make unscheduled visits to the offender's home or workplace. Some probation officers work exclusively with juvenile offenders, others with adults.

Probation and parole officers (see the following text) typically have bachelor's or master's degrees. Typical majors include behavioral sciences, social work, and criminal justice. They are given state-sponsored training and are tested for certification. Often they work as trainees for several months before being given regular employment.

Professionals in this area must be well organized to properly manage dozens of cases simultaneously. They need excellent communication skills for interacting with the diverse range of offenders they counsel. They must also have critical-thinking and decision-making skills to assess each person's needs and the appropriate resources. Officers must be levelheaded and unemotional in working with clients who may be rebellious, belligerent, or upset.

Probation and parole officers are employed by county or state governments. On average, they earn about the same as police officers and deputies. Experienced officers may advance to supervisory roles.

Parole Officers

Prisoners who are released early are assigned to supervision under parole officers. These officials perform many of the same functions as probation officers. In some jurisdictions, the same professionals serve as both probation and parole officers.

However, released prisoners face challenges that are different from those of offenders who have never served time. Successfully reentering society is often difficult, especially for former inmates who have served long terms. Besides monitoring their behavior, parole officers

Probation and parole officers meet regularly with criminal offenders who are at liberty but under supervision. An officer typically manages dozens of cases simultaneously.

help them find jobs, job training, and counseling if necessary.

Probation and parole officers supervise drug testing and maintain constant electronic monitoring of certain offenders. While their jobs are sometimes

TESTING THE CAREER WATERS

Law enforcement officers frequently encounter law-breakers. They also deal with people who, although not criminals, are disobedient and dislike authority. These individuals include people who are being sued or who have lost civil court or family court cases and are ignoring fines, restraints, or other penalties that the court imposed against them.

One part-time experience can provide a glimpse of what it's like to interact with people who might be unfriendly toward the judicial system. Process servers are responsible for hand delivering legal documents to parties involved in judicial proceedings. Many recipients dread being served papers and go to great lengths to avoid it. Some vent their resentment at the messengers who deliver the messages.

A lawyer who represents the client on the opposing side of a case usually hires a process server. Lawyers are not allowed to serve papers themselves; they must hire process servers for that task. The server must find the person (often at night or on weekends), explain what the document is, and hand it over. If the person refuses to accept it, the server can drop it at the individual's feet.

Not all legal papers provoke resistance. Process servers also deliver subpoenas that simply require third-party witnesses to appear at trials or hearings to present evidence. One encounter with a belligerent, obscenity-shouting recipient, however, may

(continued on the next page)

(continued from the previous page)

suffice to help servers decide that a job in law enforcement or legal processes is not for them.

Process servers in most states must be U.S. citizens and at least eighteen years old with no criminal record. Some states require licensing.

stressful, they are very rewarding when clients successfully return to the community.

Getting Serious About a Law Enforcement Career

Before applying for a job or enrolling in college or technical school programs, young people should learn as much about the work as they can. The best way to find out if law enforcement is for them is to talk to officers who work in the community.

The actual job search can begin while still in college or, for some jobs, in high school. Internet searches will turn up job openings within a specified geographical area. In many instances, the searcher can obtain a detailed description of the job: the employee's duties, educational requirements, required experience, and salary scale.

When applying online or by mail, the applicant will have to provide a résumé and a cover letter. A résumé is a record of a person's work history and career interests. Students' résumés can begin with their personal skills, vocational interests, and school courses or extracurricular activities that have begun to prepare them for particular career categories. A résumé is a work in progress that will continue to build and change throughout a person's lifetime. It will grow and become more impressive as the employment record begins, higher education continues, and career interests become more focused.

A short, interesting cover letter will accompany the résumé. It states why the applicant is interested in the position and feels qualified. Smart job seekers note in the cover letter the reason why they want to apply not just for any job in that career field, but for that particular job with that employer. In online applications, this is the statement that will answer the standard question, "Why are you applying for this job?"

If asked to interview for a job, the applicant should arrive at the appointment slightly ahead of time. Present a professional impression: have a neat appearance and respectful attitude, and give thoughtful and complete answers to questions. Come prepared to ask questions of the interviewer. This not only allows you to obtain clearer information about the job; it also lets the interviewer know you, the applicant, are very serious about finding just the right position.

A clean personal record is especially important for law enforcement jobs. One or two minor traffic violations or juvenile misdemeanors will not stop a career in its tracks, but multiple negative entries will raise serious concerns with hiring officials.

The primary role of community law enforcement officers is to serve all citizens by teaching and ensuring safety and making the locale a secure place to live.

Solving Problems Within the Community

Social commentators often talk about the "global society" of the twenty-first century. Via the Internet, anyone on the planet can communicate almost instantly with anyone else, no matter where in the world they are. Simultaneously, people are rediscovering the value of connecting with and participating in their local communities. Community crime is a serious problem. Solutions are not found on the global Internet; they occur within communities.

Young people have many opportunities to serve the communities in which they live and to make life better. A career in law enforcement is a noble undertaking—a great challenge, but a job that offers great personal satisfaction.

GLOSSARY

BEAT Area of regular patrol.

BREACHES Breaks or gaps, such as in security.

CIVIL LAW Law governing noncriminal matters, such as complaints between neighbors.

CONSTITUTIONAL LAW Law that comes from the authority granted by the U.S. Constitution.

CRIMINAL LAW Law governing crimes against the public.

DISPATCHER Person who receives 911 calls and refers them to emergency responders.

ETHICS Code of guidelines concerning how professionals should and should not behave.

FELON A person who has committed a serious crime that can result in a prison sentence.

FUSILLADE Shots fired at the same time or in a rapid series, usually with a small firearm.

INCARCERATION Confinement in jail or prison.

JURISDICTION Geographic area in which a law enforcement agency or court has authority.

MISDEMEANOR Minor crime usually punished by a fine, public service, or probationary sentence.

PAROLE Early release of a prisoner.

PILFERED Stolen, usually referring to inexpensive items taken a few at a time.

PROBATION Suspended sentence allowing a criminal to go free but requiring him or her to remain under supervision.

RECRUIT Newly hired police officer undergoing training.

SANCTION Form of punishment for bad behavior, such as withdrawn favors.

SUBPOENA Court order for a person to appear and testify or submit evidence.

SURVEILLANCE Careful watch or observation, such as of a suspect or a group of people.

FOR MORE INFORMATION

American Correctional Association (ACA)
206 N. Washington Street
Alexandria, VA 22314
(703) 224-0000
Website: http://www.aca.org
The ACA "shapes the future of corrections through
strong, progressive leadership." It is a professional organization for anyone who wants to
help better the justice system.

American Jail Association
1135 Professional Court
Hagerstown, MD 21740-5853
(301) 790-3930
Website: http://www.americanjail.org
The American Jail Association supports professionals who staff U.S. jails. It offers networking,
training, education, and leadership opportunities
for career corrections professionals.

American Probation and Parole Association (APPA)
P.O. Box 11910
Lexington, KY 40578-1910
(859) 244-8203
Website: http://www.appa-net.org
APPA members are actively involved with pretrial,
probation, parole, and community-based corrections. It provides training and technical assistance, including a journal, guidebooks, and
research services.

Bureau of Justice Assistance (BJA)
Office of Justice Programs

810 Seventh Street NW
Washington, DC 20531
(202) 616-6500
Website: http://www.bja.gov
Part of the U.S. Department of Justice, the BJA
supports local, state, and tribal justice systems
for the purpose of achieving safer communities.

Correctional Service Canada (CSC)
National Headquarters
340 Laurier Avenue W.
Ottawa, ON K1A 0P9
Canada
(613) 992-5891
Website: http://www.csc-scc.gc.ca
Correctional Service Canada is the Canadian
agency responsible for incarcerating and reha-
bilitating criminal offenders sentenced to at least
two years. It manages institutions of different
security levels and supervises offenders condi-
tionally released in the community.

International Association of Chiefs of Police (IACP)
44 Canal Center Plaza, Suite 200
Alexandria, VA 22314
(703) 836-6767
Website: http://www.theiacp.org
The IACP advances professional police services,
champions the recruitment and training of qualified job applicants, and encourages police
personnel worldwide "to achieve and maintain
the highest standards of ethics, integrity, community interaction, and professional conduct."

National Association of Legal Investigators (NALI)
235 N. Pine Street
Lansing, MI 48933
(866) 520-6254
Website: http://www.nalionline.org
The NALI is an association of legal professionals
investigating negligence issues for plaintiffs or
criminal defenders. Its purpose is "to educate
and advance the art and science of legal investigation, and to ensure the highest standard of
professional ethics."

Royal Canadian Mounted Police (RCMP)
Headquarters Building
73 Leikin Drive
Ottawa, ON K1A 0R2
Canada
(613) 993-7267
Website: http://www.rcmp-grc.gc.ca
The RCMP is Canada's historic national, federal,
provincial, and municipal policing organization. Its
jurisdiction includes more than 150 municipalities
and more than 600 aboriginal communities.

U.S. Bureau of Labor Statistics (BLS)
2 Massachusetts Avenue NE, Room 2850
Washington, DC 20212
(202) 691-5200
Website: http://www.bls.gov
The BLS is a U.S. Department of Labor agency
that analyzes job descriptions, salaries, growth,
demands, trends, and statistics. It publishes
the *Occupational Outlook Handbook*, which

provides information about hundreds of career fields and specific jobs.

Websites

Because of the changing nature of Internet links, Rosen Publishing has developed an online list of websites related to the subject of this book. This site is updated regularly. Please use this link to access the list:

http://www.rosenlinks.com/CIYC/Law

FOR FURTHER READING

Bickerstaff, Linda. *Careers in Undercover Narcotics Investigation* (Extreme Law Enforcement). New York, NY: Rosen Publishing, 2014.

Blackwell, Amy Hackney. *Law Enforcement and Public Safety* (Ferguson Career Launcher). New York, NY: Ferguson Publishing (Infobase Learning), 2011.

Brezina, Corona. *Careers in the Homicide Unit* (Extreme Law Enforcement). New York, NY: Rosen Publishing, 2014.

Brezina, Corona. *Careers in Law Enforcement* (Careers in Criminal Justice). New York, NY: Rosen Publishing, 2009.

Cornelio, Lisa, and Gail Eisenberg. *Public Safety, Law, and Security* (Top Careers in Two Years). New York, NY: Ferguson Publishing (Infobase Learning), 2008.

Evans, Colin. *New York Police Department* (Law Enforcement Agencies). New York, NY: Chelsea House, 2011.

Ferguson. *Law Enforcement* (Discovering Careers for Your Future). New York, NY: Ferguson Publishing, 2008.

Harmon, Daniel E. *Careers in the Corrections System* (Careers in Criminal Justice). New York, NY: Rosen Publishing, 2010.

Kamberg, Mary-Lane. *Getting a Job in Law Enforcement, Security, and Corrections* (Job Basics: Getting the Job You Need). New York, NY: Rosen Publishing, 2013.

Kanefield, Teri. *Guilty? Crime, Punishment, and the Changing Face of Justice.* Boston, MA: HMH Books, 2014.

Newton, Michael. *Crime Fighting and Crime Prevention* (Criminal Justice). New York, NY: Chelsea House, 2011.

Porterfield, Jason. *Careers in Undercover Gang Investigation* (Extreme Law Enforcement). New York, NY: Rosen Publishing, 2014.

Shone, Rob. *Crime Scene Investigators* (Graphic Forensic Science). New York, NY: Rosen Publishing, 2008.

Sterngass, Jon. *Public Safety, Law, and Security* (Great Careers with a High School Diploma). New York, NY: Facts on File, 2008.

Suen, Anastasia. *Careers with SWAT Teams* (Extreme Law Enforcement). New York, NY: Rosen Publishing, 2014.

Sutherland, Adam. *Police Forensics* (On the Radar: Defend and Protect). Minneapolis, MN: Lerner Publishing Group, 2012.

Watson, Stephanie. *A Career as a Police Officer* (Essential Careers). New York, NY: Rosen Publishing, 2010.

West, David. *Detective Work with Forensics* (Graphic Forensic Science). New York, NY: Rosen Publishing, 2008.

Woog, Adam. *Careers in State, County, and City Police Forces* (Law and Order Jobs). New York, NY: Cavendish Square Publishing, 2014.

Worth, Richard. *Los Angeles Police Department* (Law Enforcement Agencies). New York, NY: Chelsea House, 2011.

California Department of Consumer Affairs, Bureau of Security and Investigative Services. "Frequently Asked Questions—Private Investigator (PI)." 2014. Retrieved December 2, 2014 (www.bsis.ca.gov/customer_service/faqs/pi.shtml).

California Department of Fish and Wildlife. "Fish and Wildlife Officer Career." Retrieved December 2, 2014 (www.dfg.ca.gov/enforcement/career).

Chippewa Valley Technical College Associate Degree Description. "Criminal Justice—Law Enforcement." 2014. Retrieved December 2, 2014 (www.cvtc.edu/programs/program-catalog/Pages/Criminal-Justice-LE.aspx).

DegreeDirectory.org. "Highway Patrol Officer: Career Profile, Employment, and Education Requirements." 2014. Retrieved December 2, 2014 (http://degreedirectory.org/articles/Highway_Patrol_Officer_Career_Profile_Employment_Outlook_and_Education_Requirements.html).

DegreeDirectory.org. "How to Become a Highway Patrol Officer in 5 Steps." Retrieved December 2, 2014 (http://degreedirectory.org/articles/Highway_Patrol_Officer_Become_a_Highway_Patrol_Officer_in_5_Steps.html).

DegreeDirectory.org. "What Does a Wildlife Conservation Officer Do?" 2014. Retrieved December 2, 2014 (http://degreedirectory.org/articles/What_Does_a_Wildlife_Conservation_Officer_Do.html).

Discover Policing. "Opportunities for Youth in Law Enforcement." 2014. Retrieved December 2, 2014 (http://discoverpolicing.org/find_your_career/?fa=opp_young_adults).

Education Portal. "State Highway Patrol Officer: Education Requirements & Career Info." Retrieved

December 2, 2014 (http://education-portal.com/articles/Be_a_State_Highway_Patrol_Officer_Education_Requirements_and_Career_Info.html).

Loewen, Stanley C. "Becoming More Observant." HealthGuidance.org. 2014. Retrieved December 2, 2014 (www.healthguidance.org/entry/16002/1/Becoming-More-Observant.html).

Navarro, Joe. "Becoming a Great Observer." *Psychology Today SpyCatcher* blog, January 2, 2012. Retrieved December 2, 2014 (www.psychologytoday.com/blog/spycatcher/201201/becoming-great-observer).

Peterson's CollegeQuest. "How to Become a Police Officer." 2014. Retrieved December 2, 2014 (www.collegequest.com/how-to-become-a-police-officer.aspx).

PI Magazine website. "Frequently Asked Questions About Private Investigators." 2010. Retrieved December 2, 2014 (www.pimagazine.com/private_investigator_faq.htm).

PoliceLink. "The 8 Fastest Growing Law Enforcement Careers." 2014. Retrieved December 2, 2014 (http://policelink.monster.com/benefits/articles/130259-8-fastest-growing-law-enforcement-careers).

Process-Servers.net. "Is Process Serving a Good Career for You?" 2008. Retrieved December 2, 2014 (www.process-servers.net/Is-Process-Serving-a-Good-Career-for-You.asp).

Real Police Law Enforcement Resource. "Police and Law Enforcement General Job Requirements." 2014. Retrieved December 2, 2014 (www.realpolice.net/articles/training/police-and-law-enforcement-general-job-requirements.html).

The Riley Guide. "Job and Industry Resources for Law Enforcement & Protective Services Careers." 2014. Retrieved December 2, 2014 (www.rileyguide.com/protect.html).

Torpey, Elka. "You're a What? Process Server." *Occupational Outlook Quarterly*, Spring 2012. Retrieved July 2014 (www.bls.gov/opub/ooq/2012/spring/yawhat.pdf).

Wagner, David. "Radar Gun Targets Texting & Driving." *InformationWeek*, September 22, 2014. Retrieved December 2, 2014 (www.informationweek.com/it-life/radar-gun-targets-texting-and-driving/a/d-id/1315933).

Waid, Michael (correctional and security officer). Interview with the author, November 9, 2014.

Washington State Patrol. "Kiwanis Youth Law Enforcement Career Camp." 2008. Retrieved December 2, 2014 (www.wsp.wa.gov/community/kiwanis.htm).

Welch, Brian (South Carolina Department of Natural Resources officer). Interview with the author, October 24, 2014.

INDEX

C

commercial and business security officers, 50–52
correctional institutions, types of, 40–42
correctional officers
career prospects, 48
education and training, 47–48
personal traits, 46–47
what they do, 42–46
cover letters, 64, 65

D

deputies, 7, 9, 11, 31, 34, 37, 39, 52, 55, 61
detectives, police, 11, 18, 48

H

highway patrol officers/ state troopers, 9, 30–33
career preparation and prospects, 37–39

I

interviews, 65

M

maximum-security prisons, 42
medium-security prisons, 42
minimum-security prisons, 40–42

N

neighborhood watch programs, 8

O

observational skills, ways to improve, 14–15

P

parole officers, 61–64
police officers
career prospects, 18
education and training, 16–17
personal traits and requirements, 13–16
what they do, 7–13
private investigators
career prospects, 28–29
legal authority, 25, 28–29
personal traits, 25
training and experience, 26–27
what they do, 21–25

probation officers,
60–61, 62
process servers, 63–64
public sites, security
officers at, 52

R

résumés, 64–65

S

security agencies, 53–54
security officers
career prospects, 59
education and training,
58–59
personal traits and skills,
57–58

and security agencies,
53–54
types of, 50–53
state troopers/highway
patrol officers, 9,
30–33
career preparation and
prospects, 37–39
store detectives, 52–53

W

Waid, Michael, 45, 54,
56–57
Welch, Brian, 36–37
wildlife officers, 6, 33–37
career preparation and
prospects, 37–39

About the Author

Daniel E. Harmon is the author of more than 90 books. His career studies volumes for Rosen Publishing include *Careers in the Corrections System* (Careers in Criminal Justice) and *Careers in Explosives and Arson Investigation* (Careers in Forensics). He has also written books on military intelligence, the Federal Bureau of Investigation, and the office of U.S. attorney general. A veteran editor and writer, he has contributed thousands of articles to national and regional magazines, newspapers, and newsletters. In his spare time, he writes historical crime fiction. Harmon lives in Spartanburg, South Carolina.

Photo Credits

Cover © iStockphoto.com/Susan Chiang; p. 5 Huntstock/Thinkstock; pp. 8, 56 Photo Researchers/Science Source/Getty Images; p. 10 moodboard/Thinkstock; p. 12 PeopleImages.com/DigitalVision/Getty Images; p. 16 Stockbyte/Thinkstock; p. 20 Don Bayley/E+/Getty Images; p. 22 ballyscanlon/Photographer's Choice RF/Getty Images; p. 23 rj lerich/Shutterstock.com; p. 27 © Jeff Cook/Quad-City Times/ZUMA Press p. 31 Ariel Skelley/Blend Images/Getty Images; p. 32 William Silver/Shutterstock.com; p. 34 meunierd/Shutterstock.com; p. 38 Blend Images/Shutterstock.com; p. 41 Press Association/AP Images; p. 44 © AP Images; p. 47 RJ Sangosti/Denver Post/Getty Images; p. 49 Jon Feingersh/Blend Images/Getty Images; p. 51 Stockbyte/Thinkstock; p. 54 bikeriderlondon/Shutterstock.com; p. 57 Mario Tama/Photonica World/Getty Images; p. 62 Lisa F. Young/Shutterstock.com; p. 66 Peter Dazeley/Iconica/Getty Images; cover and interior pages border and background images © iStockphoto.com/ScottTalent (fingerprint), © iStockphoto.com/Pingebat (map).

Designer: Nicole Russo; Editor: Heather Moore Niver; Photo Researcher: Sherri Jackson